T0148561

RHYTHM
of the
FATHER'S HEART

LIFE LEARNING CLASS REMOVING THE LAYERS

JIMMY MITCHELL

WESTBOW®
PRESS
A DIVISION OF THOMAS NELSON
& ZONDERVAN

Scripture taken from the New King James Version. Copyright © 1979, 1980,
1982 by Thomas Nelson, Inc. Used by permission. All rights reserved.

Scripture taken from the King James Version of the Bible.

WestBow Press books may be ordered through booksellers or by contacting:

WestBow Press
A Division of Thomas Nelson & Zondervan
1663 Liberty Drive
Bloomington, IN 47403
www.westbowpress.com
1 (866) 928-1240

ISBN: 978-1-4908-7549-1 (sc)
ISBN: 978-1-4908-7550-7 (e)

Library of Congress Control Number: 2015905170

Print information available on the last page.

WestBow Press rev. date: 12/9/2015

Are you hurt, confused, frustrated, and just plain tired? Have you found yourself repeatedly traveling the same path? In spite of your best efforts and well-meaning intentions, you always seem to end up in the same place. Even in your relationships, you're stuck in a meaningless cycle and can't seem to move forward. Frustration creeps in, while others around you seem to have it all together. Watching other's exhibit what you desire for yourself, only adds to your frustration. Even when you acquire that elusive something—additional income, new car, new house, or a new relationship—for a moment, things feel good. They feel right. You look around at what you have acquired and feel you're finally moving ahead.

Then, like clockwork, those old feelings of lack and limitation find their way back into your life, and the cycle repeats itself. Once again, your internal dialogue controls your thoughts, and you feel like a failure. Believing the voices in your head, you begin to act like a failure, and you return to what you have always done because that's all you know. Failure becomes familiar, and you settle for the person *you* created—not the person the Father (God) created.

Let us stop the cycle of self-doubt by reprogramming the dialogue in your head and examining the layers that have defined your life.

Welcome to Life Learning Class: removing the layers one layer at a time!

WHAT IS RHYTHM?

R hythm has been described as "a regular pattern of movement or beat; a pattern of systemic flow." These patterns of occurrences can vary from seconds to thousands of years. One such example of this phenomenon is the seasons—winter, spring, summer, and fall. Within these seasons (flow), we find additional rhythms and patterns of movement: planting (seedtime), germination, and harvesting.

People have patterns and cycles too. The key is to identify the season we are in. If it is seedtime in one particular area of our life, we will not be fruitful trying to harvest. How will we know what season we are in? We will know through prayer and exploration. At some point, we have to start exploring (digging) to find and develop (work) the season we are in, observing what is happening in the moment. Recognize, also, that we can be in more than one season simultaneously; we can be planting in one area of our life while harvesting in another. Going to the next level will first entail mastery of the current level, a harvest (the conclusion of a process), and then seedtime (the beginning of a new process). We must be very aware of our rhythm and stay connected to the Father. He is always communicating with us; He will guide us through any situation. Stay alert and attentive to His leading, for life sets up traps; life always presents opportunities for our learning and growth.

What Is the Rhythm of the Father's (God's) Heart?

First, we must recognize that the Father is love itself. This may be a hard concept for some, but He is love! The Father's rhythm is a repeated pattern (flow) of unconditional and unwavering love. His love never changes; it is constant, and it is true. The Father will never withhold His love (Himself) from us. He loves us so much He made us the object of His love (affection). As a result of His undeniable love for us, He deposited an extension of Himself (love) within us to nurture and share.

For God so loved the world that He gave His
only begotten Son, that whoever believes in Him
should not perish but have everlasting life.
—John 3:16 (NKJV)

Beloved, let us love one another, for love is of God; and
everyone who loves is born of God and knows God. He
who does not love does not know God, for God is love.
—1 John 4:7–8 (NKJV)

In His unequivocal wisdom, the Father understood
the frailty of the human condition. He understood that
we would need help in nurturing (developing) His gift
of love, so He provided Himself—just a conversation
(prayer) away. Then, as a constant reminder, He gave us
the reassurance. "I will never leave thee, nor forsake thee"
(Hebrews 13:5).

When we are in alignment with God (love), we have
an innate desire to share (flow) the gifts we have inside
of us. It was always God's plan for us to respect the order
(structure) He created and to remain in alignment with
Him. He wants us to have a relationship; to have intimacy
with Him (reciprocating His love); and to seek Him
always in prayer, through praise, reading His word, and
quiet introspective time with Him.

The diagram below depicts the intended relationship with God. In right order, there are intensely passionate moments that a bride and groom share. The intensity of these moments should mirror the passionate relationship that one shares with God. As the head of the household, males need to first understand their role, embrace this concept, and treat their wives accordingly. This will allow a woman's nourishing nature to flourish both to her husband and to her children. Don't misconstrue this statement. It is not the physical nature of these moments that is important but the intensity of the connection. One must still have a pure heart. From the purity of the union, love will flow down to the children, who shall also see and love God. From there, the ministry can flow.

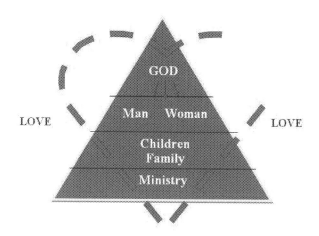

Blessed are the pure in heart: for they shall see God.
—Matthew 5:8 (KJV)—

WHAT IS LOVE?

L ove is an emotion. It is an affectional intelligence. Affectional intelligence is the capacity to be influenced by a place, object, or situation. We determine the extent, intensity, and length of the connection. People increase their affectional intelligence by how they manage their feelings.

We are spirit beings living out human experiences on this plane: earth. To be a human being is to have emotion. God created us and gave us emotion. Emotion (love), as intended by God, is good. Please be careful not to confuse the Father's love with worldly love. It can be easy to misinterpret the two. One is free while the other often comes with a price.

Emotions are sometimes classified as positive or negative, and in doing so, we may feel the need to try to suppress them. Why are we unable or unwilling to express them in a healthy way? There are a couple of reasons why this might be the case. First, we were not given permission to do so. second, if we did, we felt condemned. In one way or another, we have all experienced the anguish of emotions, the race through past hurts, present inadequacies, verbal attacks, rising tensions, losing control, the possibility of physical violence, and the potential to hurt the very one(s) we love.

It is common for people to associate the Father's ability to love them with the love experiences they have received from family and friends, but they are definitely not the same. Earthly love is usually shrouded in conditions. God's love is free, constant, and true. The depth and degree of the relationship with the Father always remains with us. The Father always wants to see His children happy. He wants to give us the desires of our heart; He is just waiting for us to arrive at the appropriate level of maturity (relationship) with Him. "His thoughts are not our thoughts, neither are his ways our ways" (Isaiah 55:8–9).

> But seek ye first the kingdom of God,
> and his righteousness; and all these
> things shall be added unto you.
> —Matthew 6:33 (KJV)

People are impatient; we want what we want when we want it. This expectation of immediacy in receiving has become so rampant that it has been dubbed "the microwave generation." Many Christians are not an exception. When we pray and make a petition to God and it is not fulfilled on our timetable, we assume we are out of favor with God. It cannot be overstated that God does not delight in withholding from His children. He is waiting on our maturity and obedience.

For example, you have been giving your eight-year-old some basic principles of driving. Each time he goes in the vehicle, he watches you diligently and asks very intelligent and mature questions. After several months of watching and gathering information, he asks you for the keys to your Mercedes. Would you give him the keys? Of course, the answer is no! But he has prayed and praised God in worship, he has worked hard, and he has been an exceptional student. He is confident in his mastery of the vehicle, he has memorized the traffic signals and directional signs, he meets the height requirement, and he knows that he can handle himself, so why not? Outside of the obvious, it is illegal. You (in your *maturity*) know that he is not mentally or emotionally mature enough to navigate the impending onslaught of movement and information he will have to process while driving.

There is that word again: *maturity!* You know in time that he will reach maturity and reap the reward. But that doesn't change the fact that the decision is for his protection, not to deny or punish him. It is the same with the Father. His understanding of where we are and what we need is on a much greater level than we are capable of understanding. Trust Him! "His thoughts are not our thoughts, neither are our ways his ways" (Isaiah 55:8–9).

WHERE DO MOST PEOPLE GET THEIR CONCEPT OF LOVE?

Our concept of love often develops during our formative years, while we are still quite young. Usually our parents or caregivers provide us with our initial concept of love. Of course, siblings, grandparents, and other family members play an integral part in influencing us. Later on, teachers, clergy, neighbors, and others will also have an impact on our life. If these experiences were positive, our "love outlook" will be positive, but if we had negative experiences, the way we view love will be negative. For example, if we are performance oriented, we will work hard to reach our goal, which is ultimately to receive praise, even if it means distorting the truth and our authentic self (the person we were created to be). The more we engage in this practice the more we move away from our true self. This is not necessarily a conscious behavior. Many become performance oriented out of a need to win a parent or caregiver's approval or avoid that person's wrath. This pattern becomes a carved pathway that limits our ability to pour (flow) into others. Repetition of the behavior creates a long-lasting habit, so we tend to approach each situation in the same manner.

A variety of material has been published about the subject of love and its origin and meaning. But information about learning to love through our senses, which is embedded at a cellular level, is not as widespread. We associate love to a person, encounter, or experience. If we have a negative experience where someone hurts us, that person's name (hearing) or things associated with that person—cologne (smell), physical attributes (sight), being forced to eat something you dislike (taste,) being struck (touch), and so on—can quite easily be internalized negatively. This information is then stored in our neurons (nerve cells). Subsequently, if the person genuinely expresses a kind gesture toward us, it is difficult for us to accept. Our internal dialogue says they really mean us harm.

In an attempt to avoid repeated trauma, a seemingly logical response is not to talk about it in a productive manner or to bury it. We think this makes it go away. Be assured, it does not go away. We retain the information in our neurons, in our memory, and in our subconscious. From there it continues to place restraints on our lives. For example, many women have difficulty in relationships with males because of a breakdown in their relationship with their father. Likewise, many males struggle with relating to women because of a poor relationship with their mother. These are just two of many combinations of damaged male and female relationships that can affect us. Unfortunately, much of the time, we do not determine the origin of our pain, so healing is deferred and in some cases never occurs. It is in identifying the source of the pain and shifting the internal dialogue that activates change, and then our deliverance will come. Holding onto the pain hurts *us*, not the other person. Forgiveness of the offender and ourselves is key to our complete healing.

Operating Outside of the Father's Rhythm (Plan)

Attitudes and behaviors outside of the Father's plan can wreak all sorts of havoc in the home and societally. God designed an order, a balance, and a hierarchy. When we disregard *His order,* things become misaligned, His flow to us becomes interrupted, and additional unnecessary steps ensue.

For example, if a father is absent and a child is raised primarily by females, without a predominant male in the equation, there is a greater probability that the child will have an imbalanced understanding of authority. This is a very common occurrence within many households today, but certainly an absentee mother also interrupts the normal internal dialogue that should occur within a child. Please note: "absentee parent" references not only those outside of the home, but also those absentee (noncontributing) parents who live within the household.

An equally challenging scenario arises when the female minimizes the male's role in the household and makes the child her primary focus. This determines what the child sees as normal and appropriate behavior within a household. If the child's understanding of parental roles is not corrected, his or her misunderstanding becomes a precursor for another generation of imbalanced behavior.

Many of today's grandparents have been thrust into the role of being parents once again, and some individuals have simply become self–absorbed and have no interest or desire to assume their (grand) parenting role. In either case, what should be a natural evolution of teaching and learning (an imparting of wisdom) is hindered, if not lost.

Finally, we look at well-meaning parents who want their child to have a better (different) upbringing than they had. For instance, a household in which a child has input and his or her opinions are valued and strongly influence how the household is run.

While this scenario has the potential to be positive (open parent-child communication is healthy), too often the sound structure (boundaries) and societal norms fundamental to the parent's upbringing are eliminated from their child's upbringing, such as regular chores, limited use of electronic devices, reading, respecting adults, and so on. If we address this with many of today's parents, they will have a litany of reasons (excuses) why they parent in this way. This is called "denial" and is an avoidance behavior, but it can only be avoided for so long. Children require sound and consistent structure.

Prematurely giving a child access to adult decisions and processes is problematic. What should be a steady, progressive transition from childhood to adulthood becomes accelerated. This results in a society of adult-looking, emotionally hindered young people who are not equipped to handle the daily demands of the adult world. There is an epidemic of people unable to cope. Have you noticed the suicide rate among the youth has skyrocketed? This is no coincidence. Briefly, let us look at some stats from the Centers for Disease Control and

Prevention (CDC). Suicide is the third leading cause of death among persons aged fifteen to twenty-four, the second among persons aged twenty-five to thirty-four, the fourth among persons aged thirty-five to fifty-four, and the eighth among persons fifty-five to sixty-four.

Please do not infer the converse is true. It is not being suggested that healthy and upstanding children cannot be raised from these scenarios. Neither is it being suggested that we are bad parents if any part of these scenarios apply—we all do the best we know how. What is being proposed is that children raised under these conditions have more challenges to face and conquer. Why saddle them with unnecessary baggage? If we repeatedly try to address a behavior(s) and do not observe a change, we should seek advice. There is no shame in seeking help, the challenge is when we know there is a problem and do nothing. Love and nurture children through the principles set forth by God. Prepare them—life is tough enough as it is. Let us work to stop the cycle of imbalanced relationships!

What is your love language? First, let's look at a definition of love language. I believe it is a body of words and the system of how we use it, common to people who are of the same community or nation—the same geographical area or same cultural tradition. A person or group communicating by voice, a distinctive vibrational expression through a culture's formalized system of words, sounds, and gestures. There is one rhythm of love, one continuous love language. It is a matter of how it is expressed in the community, country, family, or body of people. It is the manifestation of thoughts, words, gestures, and language with the intent of evoking a favorable response from the intended subject.

What does love look like? As youngsters, our initial love language is formulated whether good or bad. If the experiences were loving and joyful, the face of love will be positive; conversely, if we were raised in a stressful and anger-filled environment, our impression of love will be negative. Equally important, a household with disengaged parents, who are reserved in their expression of love, will foster a child who concludes this to be appropriate behavior and internalizes this misrepresented interpretation of what love should look like. The degree to which love is present or lacking will strongly influence how that child navigates life. Over the course of time, when a child doesn't receive healthy expressions of love, he or she will develop a poor self-image and be prone to a lifetime of relational challenges.

When someone communicates love to a receiver dealing with issues of hurt, the information received will be skewed, because the receiver's pain inhabits his or her ability to receive the true intent of the communicator. The same is true if the communicator has issues of hurt; the way he or she communicates will often be negative and hurtful. Hurt people will often hurt people. For example, an abandoned person, whether through neglect, adoption, or parental disengagement, will have negatively impacted self-esteem, which in turn hinders that person's love language, first toward himself or herself and then toward others.

How would you view love? If you are the above-mentioned person, hurt by abandonment, how would you respond to giving or even receiving love? We know from numerous studies on this subject that if a person's basic needs are not met, he or she is unable to adequately navigate to the next level of development. The basic needs of water, food, shelter, and rest, along with security and safety should be realized before the natural progression to love occurs. Without the actualization of these initial needs, what would the face of love look like? The face of love will be the face of that individual who is influencing and molding you and creating your interpretation of love. That could be a parent, guardian, or family member—whoever has the overwhelming impact on you as your initial love language is being formulated. The formulated expression of love is then carried into subsequent relationships, where often, the behavior will be to fight the person in front of you rather than fighting the erroneous image of love. The emotions that came on the days of abandonment are carved into your mind and cause you to distrust others and often yourself. You then move seamlessly from cycle to cycle.

Do you know who influenced your love language? Take a few minutes and travel back in time to your younger self. Identify who had great influence in your life. Can you determine if the influence had a positive or negative impact on you? If you are unsure, as you think about this individual, take note of how you feel inside. Are you emoting happy and positive feelings, or do you feel sad, dread, or even fear? This is a good indicator of how you may have internalized love. Of course, we understand that more than one individual can contribute to the formulization of your love language, but usually there is a predominate individual who influences us. We also recognize that trauma can override an initially well-laid love language. We unpackaged this further in a subsequent chapter.

Love is both a noun and a verb. A person can be the object of love as well as the subject of love. One of the most cherished and misunderstood things are the subject of love. When we enter a new relationship, we eagerly gather information to determine all the things we think we have in common, but this is usually a superficial analysis at best. As we spend more time with one another and the exploration delves deeper, we expose what had been long rooted within us—our belief system. What we believe determines how we negotiate in relationships, good or bad. Restoration of a healthy love language and becoming rooted and grounded in authentic love—its language, face, sound, and gestures—are so important to our happiness and self-actualization (**see Ephesians 3:17**). **That Christ may dwell in your hearts by faith; that ye, being rooted and grounded in love**. Love was designed to be a beautiful and nurturing thing. Pay attention to your current relationship(s). If you find yourself attracting the same types of unhealthy relationships or operating in undesirable behavioral patterns, it can usually be traced back to a learned behavior from an imbalanced relationship. A time when someone of influence misguided or mistreated you, which impeded your development. Therefore, now you love from the place in which you are stuck. What we think about love now sets things in motion and causes us to project our future, and what we believe will happen will come true.

If we live without consciousness, we will continually recreate our pasts—recreate the very thing we say we do not want. Our futures will look just like our pasts. We will attract the same experiences in our relationships and end up in the same place. Many females have been known to say that all men are dogs, yet they enter and remain in relationships with that mind-set, hoping for more, but not expecting more than a "dog" mentality from their mates. On the other hand, we have men who pursue women primarily because of their physical attributes. They are more interested in bragging rights and impressing their friends than creating sound and healthy relationships. Sadly, deep down they really want a woman to love and respect.

Again, we increase our affectional intelligence by how we manage our "feelings" process. Becoming conscious of the process is key. The range of what we think and do is limited by what we fail to notice.

Nothing will change until we stop ignoring the signs and take notice of what shapes our thoughts and actions. By observing our external life, we understand what occurs in our internal life (revelatory experience). Self-observation shows how we developed the concept of love.

Have You Made Observations
of the Cycles in Your Life?

Sometimes without thinking, we speak. Without reflecting, we act. Without looking, we assume to see. Without listening, we make a reply. When this occurs, the information we operate out of is erroneous; however, we assume the information we gathered is accurate. This pattern of behavior disrupts and distorts the flow of what should have occurred. It becomes important to unpack the components of our behavior to expose an opportunity for corrective measures and healing.

We can control our thoughts, but we cannot stop the emotion. When we ask someone, "How do you feel?" about another person's behavior, more often than not that person tells us what he or she thinks. Here is an example for clearer understanding. Bruce and Amanda are having an argument. If you ask Amanda how Bruce's comment made her feel, more than likely she will respond, "I feel like what Bruce said was wrong because …" Notice she has not answered the question "How did it make *you* feel?" We truly need to separate our thoughts from our feelings, but understand that our feelings are just as important and valid as our thoughts.

When we see particularly concerning behavior(s) in our children, more than likely we will have to look deeper than their surface behaviors. Often their behaviors are indicative of a greater issue, an expression of an unmet need. Admittedly, at times, their behavior can be one of manipulation because they want something we have denied. We are not referring to those occasions; this is normal childlike behavior (and should be expected). We need to closely examine the deep-rooted anger outbursts, fits of rage, silent treatment, signs of depression, and so on. For these, somewhere an unmet need is dictating an aspect of their life. For many, this is not always a conscious process, children (and adults) can have feelings of misalignment (failure, unpopularity, being misunderstood, and so forth) and don't have the words to appropriately articulate how they feel, so it manifests in behaviors. Please note, sometimes what we perceive as the child's unmet need is actually our own. Parents have been known to try to live vicariously through their children, projecting their own desires and dreams upon the children, which can cause rebellion.

We must take note of our children's natural tendencies and nurture them, not break them. For example, a three-year-old constantly takes pens and markers and writes on walls and everywhere but where she should. For many parents, the natural tendency would be to get upset and punish the child. While corrective instruction is necessary, encouraging her behavior is a healthy way: implement a reward system for writing in the designated places. Look deeper, beyond the obvious (defaced walls), and see that he may be expressing an innate creativity. This could be an early expression of his future as a literary Nobel Prize recipient. When we look at it from this prospective, his actions seem less offensive.

Many of us can recant childhood stories of enjoying one activity or another that our parents deemed idle or foolish and discouraged us from doing. This quite possibly could have been a seed designed to be nurtured and shared with humankind. This quite possibly could have been the very thing for which we would be most passionate about and that would provide us with a sense of purpose. For some, we will eventually reconnect with that seed, but for others, the dream will be lost. Look around. Countless people are in good jobs and making good money, yet they are miserable because they are not passionate and don't feel fulfilled.

> For every tree is known by his own fruit
> —Luke 6:44 (KJV)

The scripture indicate that if we examine the fruit, we should be able to know which tree it's from, e.g. acorns should have been produced by an oak. Behavior is fruit of the thought, so if we look at our behavior (fruit), we can know our thought (tree). It will take the Father or a trained (anointed) individual to help us recalibrate how we examine our thoughts and behaviors.

What is the condition of your tree (life)? What fruit does it bear?

What Is Destiny? Destiny is the "inner purpose of a life that is discovered and realized." Discovering our divine destinies and realizing (accomplishing) what God has called us to achieve is the most important thing we can ever do; it's why we were born. Renewing our mind and transforming our thinking from the world's point of view to God's point of view will enable us to fulfill our destinies.

Destiny is the powerful and irresistible force of something that is foreordained (appoint, determine, designate, assign) and evokes our greatness and our noble course in life, and it manifests our God-given purpose.

Many are seeking their life's purpose. The scripture states:

For every one that asketh receiveth; and he that seeketh findeth; and to him that knocketh it shall be opened
—Matthew 7:8 (KJV)

What Is My Purpose?

Once you ask the question, it is necessary to stay quiet, available, receptive, and patient. Allow the rhythm of the Father's heart to supply the correct response. Admittedly, the response may not come as quickly as we may like. While at other times, it will come almost simultaneously with the question. We must pay attention to our reoccurring thoughts, feelings, words, and images. In the process, it is essential to move away from judgment. We must give ourselves permission not to know what we have never known in order to know what we have never known.

We each have a unique gift—it just needs to be unwrapped. Each gift is valuable and has its own expression, so it is futile to strive to pattern our behavior, our life, exactly after another person. We are to maintain our individuality. We are to be proud of who God has made us to be. We are here to be of service to humanity. It is destined. If we do not know our purposes, it is important to seek God. He will reveal it to us. Do not be distracted by another person's journey or become disenfranchised by his or her successes—celebrate with that person. Someone's success does not minimize who we are; we are all equally important—an essential member of the body of Christ.

Why Are We Here Today? We are really here today to begin the process of unlearning to:

- ✓ unpack some baggage
- ✓ get to the core of who we were created to be
- ✓ learn to co-create (co-labor) our world with God
- ✓ examine sabotaging behaviors that we believe "are us."

Daily, we do at least a portion of what God called us to do, but we may not recognize it because it does not have an affixed title or label. What do you do on a daily basis? For example, a construction worker assigned by God to be a teacher finds himself consistently training or giving instruction to the more than twenty people that he works with. If you ask him if he thinks he is a teacher, chances are he would say no, because the label teacher or trainer is not affixed to his job description. Yet daily he has an internal drive to impart information unto others and has a desire for them to understand the information. Note, because we are called (anointed) to perform a particular duty does not mean we will not become frustrated from time to time; after all, we are human.

When we operate in our purposes with intention, the results will look different than when we do it unconsciously. If we just stop and examine it, we will realize God truly does have a purpose for our life and it is on a grander scale than we realize or could have ever imagined. It is in His plan that we find fulfillment. If we can move beyond the need to get approval and perform the task in excellence, we will have the greatest fulfillment. We should do what is right because it is right, not because it feels right.

We enter this world already called,

> For we are laborers together with God: ye are
> God's husbandry, ye are God's building.
> —1 Corinthians 3:9 (KJV)

> *When we think what we think,*
> then *do we do what we think we do,*
> or *do we do,*
> then *think about what we have done.*

(Translation: When we are conscious of our thoughts, do our actions then follow our thoughts, or do we act and then think about what we have done?) We must work to truly become present in the moment and conscious of our thoughts and actions.

What Is Your Pattern? First, what is a pattern? A pattern is the regular and repeated way in which something happens or is done. It is designed or shaped to serve as a guide. It is the template that God used when creating us. Once He produced the prototype of man, He did not have to repeat this process. In similar fashion, our spiritual experience and union with God should follow a regular pattern. As we encode information, we also exercise patterns, so memory can be a blessing as well as a curse. Memory saves us from having to relearn everything. However, this can be why we keep having the same negative experiences. We may need to unlearn something or alter our perspective.

We have patterns of behavior in response to emotional, mental and spiritual stimuli. We must be aware of the stimuli that impacts us and produces other types of manifestations (patterns) such as criminal, avoidance, and sexual patterns, there is little we can do to change. This is why we continue to produce the same responses and form the same patterns that filter all incoming information. We make all our decisions out of these patterns. If we can stop long enough to recognize our patterns, we will see the repetition in our decisions, such as financial, behavioral, relational, and so on. Of course, our focus is on changing the negative mind-sets that sabotage, injure, disable, and cripple us.

Terms to remember:

Manifest—to make evident, revealing in physical or literal form, that which was concealed in its invisible form.

Behavior—a fruit of a belief. Belief in a simple form is thought. Our thoughts suggest our beliefs, and that's why we behave in the manner that we do. Self-observation reveals how we develop the concept of love.

Manipulation—to control or play upon by artful, unfair, or insidious means especially to one's own advantage.

Mind-Set—a fixed mental attitude or disposition that predetermines a person's response or interpretation of a situation. Between a stimulus and a response there is a space. In that space is our freedom and power to choose our response. In those choices are growth and happiness.

So what is inside us? As we continue, be reminded we are each special and hold a unique destiny!

Mind—What Is It? Taber's Cyclopedic Medical Dictionary defines mind as the "integration and organization of functions of the brain resulting in the ability to perceive surroundings, to have emotions, imagination, memory and will and to process information in an intelligent manner. The quantity and quality of the functions of the mind vary with experience and development.[1]" To perceive our surroundings, would it not take our five senses?

The brain is a large mass of soft nervous tissue made up of both neurons and glial cells (provide support and protection to neurons) lying within the cranium of the skull. The brain contains both gray and white matter. This matter consists of nerve cells that gather information.[2] All these functions regulate and coordinate body activity. It is the seat of consciousness—thought, memory, reason, judgment, and emotion.

Sensory impulses are received through a nerve called afferent (nerve fiber), which registers as sensation. This is the basis for perception. Associative memory can be found in the neural net. Explanation: With each event we encounter, our senses can play an integral part in linking emotion to various aspects of the event, such as time of year, fragrance (smell), songs, temperature (feeling), clothes (sight), and so on. Have you ever noticed that a particular song, perfume/cologne, meal, or article of clothing can bring forth memories of a relationship, friend, or loved one? And, if more than one sense becomes involved in your memory, how your thought takes on greater intensity? How we processed the emotions when they first occurred is how we view our feelings.

And do not be conformed to this world,
but be transformed by the renewing of your

mind, that you may prove what is that good
and acceptable and perfect will of God.
—Romans 12:2 (NKJV)

Many believe that one of the greatest gifts to the body of Christ is Eugene Peterson's, *The Message* Bible. In it he said this:

"So here's what I want you to do, God helping you; take your every day, ordinary life— your sleeping, eating, going- to-work, and walking - around life — and place it before God as an offering. Embracing what God does for you is the best thing you can do for him. Don't become so well adjusted to your culture that you fit into it without even thinking. Instead, fix your attention on God. You'll be changed from the inside out. Readily recognize what he wants from you, and quickly respond to it. Unlike the culture around you, always dragging you down to its level of immaturity, God brings the best out of you, develops well-formed maturity in you."

I beseech you therefore, brethren by the mercies
of God that ye present your bodies a living
sacrifice holy acceptable unto god which is your
reasonable service and be not conformed to this
world; but be ye transformed by the renewing

of you mind, that ye may proved what is that
good and acceptable and perfect will of God.
—Roman 12:1–2 (KJV)

Story One:

After a failed marriage, Andre decided to go back
to school. He married out of rebellion. He knew the
marriage was going to fail but married nonetheless. In
time, he decided to move on and further his education.
He applied for a Pell Grant to attend NC State University,
which was approved. Andre had a daughter, Sandy. He
knew he must balance taking care of her and attending
school. Excited at the prospect of starting school, he told
his mother about his impending future. His mother's
response wasn't what he expected: "You know you don't
have enough faith to go to school and take care of Sandy,
as well as all your other responsibilities."

Heartbroken and discouraged, Andre dropped out
even before he began. He got a job at a local radio station
as a salesman. A salesman position would allow Andre to
travel and met new people. He was excited, but his salary
was based on commission. His mother wasn't satisfied
and commented that he needed a job with a steady
income, one that would provide a weekly paycheck. Again
disheartened, he walked away from the opportunity and
took a job in a fast-food restaurant. There he had a steady

income, but the job had no advancement opportunity, so he just made money. He did not grow or feel fulfilled.

Eventually, Andre decided to try again and take night classes at a community college. Mother insisted work, as Sandy and night classes would be too demanding. This time, in spite of her protests, he enrolled in night classes.

After many months, Andre landed a much better job as a production planner, a job he really liked. He called to share the great news with family. They were anything but enthusiastic. "You will be working long hours and have to work during the summer; besides, you don't have any training in that area." Doubt-filled, Andre took the position and started off doing a good job, but soon he began to hang out with coworkers who just did enough to get by. While management told him of his great potential, he was unable to see his authentic self. Criticism and negative thoughts rose inside of him. He just didn't see the potential that others saw in him.

This occurred in the 70s when computers were huge, audacious machines that had circuit boards. Andre had an innate knack to predict how long it would take for the computer to have a malfunction; he could even predict the area/part that would become defective. The company knew he was a great asset. However, the people Andre hung out with couldn't celebrate him or his talents, and soon he began to do as they did—just enough.

Andre was offered a transfer to another city where he could start all over, earn a good income, and improve his standard of living. After a few weeks there, the cycle repeated itself and he began to associate with coworkers who did just enough.

People don't necessarily say and react in this way to hold us back; they think they are supporting or protecting us. While others are very aware of our progression and behave in a way to protect the predictable world that we share with them. They just don't want to see us move forward for fear of being left behind.

What happens when someone close to you is overprotective like Andre's mother? His mother's responses communicated, "I really don't think you are capable of success; you are going to fail, so why try." In reality, she was projecting her fears of Andre leaving her, which Andre also came to internalize.

Andre allowed his mother to sabotage his vision. The heart knows things that the mind has yet to receive. In his heart he could see the vision for his life but knew it would meet with opposition from his family.

How many of us, like Andre, have not challenged ourselves because that would mean simultaneously challenging our parents or an authority figure?

In striving for success, many people have no idea how to promote others. To do so, they would have to step outside themselves and learn to trust. Because they are emotionally unavailable to us, we have to possess the confidence and ability to celebrate ourselves and our accomplishments, regardless of what others may say or think. We have to make a choice to be real, not defined by what someone else wants us to be. It can be the fear of our own potential for success that may be too great and presents challenges. What is the challenge? The challenge is to see ourselves where we are. Getting support from the people in our life can be tough, especially when nothing significant may be happening in their life. If we seek value from them and it can't be given, it may be because they are feeling devalued and/or lost in our accomplishments. What will it mean for them if we stay where we are versus if we leave? In Andre's case, his mother loved him, but her view of success was limited, and many of the opportunities available to him would mean she might no longer have control of his life.

Story Two:

On occasion Janice would approach Sam in a manner that gave him the impression she was seeking advice. Janice's behavior and patterns were mysterious and secretive. Through observation Sam soon came to understand she used this tactic to lure people in. Her body language expressed "I am a victim," and her dialogue was vague and deceptive, which left people lost and trying to figure out what she was trying to communicate. One had to pull the information out of her. This form of sabotaging behavior was designed to control the energy of those around her. She would lure those who did not know her into feeling sorry for her, and then she had them just where she wanted them. She was now directing them. Aloof behavior can hinder important occurrences from taking place. Through her manipulation, Janice forfeited access to vital information that others desired to give her. Janice's natural eyes could only perceive a natural understanding. Her sabotaging behavior will not end until she acknowledges spiritual understanding and the plan God has for her.

After reading these two stories, can we understand how important it is for us to stay alert? These serendipitous moments will occur regularly, but we have to notice them. Moments in our life make us feel like we need to run, but in doing so, we run toward God. In our running we may discover that which will take us into a new dimension of God.

References

1. *The Free Dictionary, s.v.* "Rhythm accessed September 15, 2013" *http://www.thefreedictionary.com/rhythm.*

2. "Suicide Facts at a Glance," *CDC Violence Prevention. Centers for Disease Control and Prevention*: *http://www.cdc.gov/ViolencePrevention/pdf/Suicide-DataSheet-a.pdf* (September 15, 2013).

3. *Dictionary.com, s.v.* "language," accessed September 15, 2013, http://dictionary.reference.com/browse/language?s=t.

4. "Will Durant > Quotes," *Goodreads. http://www.goodreads.com/author/quotes/16184.Will_Durant* (September 15, 2013).

5. Kahlil Gibran, "The Prophet." *http://www-personal.umich.edu/~jrcole/gibran/prophet/prophet.htm* (September 17, 2013).

6. *Merriam-Webster*, s.v. "pattern," accessed September 21, 2013, *http://www.merriam-webster.com/dictionary/pattern.*

7. *Taber's Cyclopedic Medical Dictionary* (Philadelphia: F.A. Davis Company, 1989)1224.

Printed in the United States
By Bookmasters